Animal Babies

Bunnies

by Kelsey Jopp

I0881246

FOCUS READERS
SCOUT

www.focusreaders.com

Copyright © 2020 by Focus Readers, Lake Elmo, MN 55042. All rights reserved. No part of this book may be reproduced or utilized in any form or by any means without written permission from the publisher.

Focus Readers is distributed by North Star Editions:
sales@northstareditions.com | 888-417-0195

Produced for Focus Readers by Red Line Editorial.

Photographs ©: DamianKuzdak/iStockphoto, cover, 1; Olha Sem/Shutterstock Images, 4; Cait Eire/Shutterstock Images, 7; gurineb/iStockphoto, 9, 16 (top left); Antonia Giroux/Shutterstock Images, 11; KQW/Shutterstock Images, 13, 16 (bottom left), 16 (bottom right); stanley45/iStockphoto, 15; MidwestWilderness/iStockphoto, 16 (top right)

Library of Congress Cataloging-in-Publication Data
Names: Jopp, Kelsey, 1993- author.
Title: Bunnies / by Kelsey Jopp.
Description: Lake Elmo, MN : Focus Readers, [2020] | Series: Animal babies | Audience: K to Grade 3. | Includes index.
Identifiers: LCCN 2018053614 (print) | LCCN 2018055850 (ebook) | ISBN 9781641859509 (pdf) | ISBN 9781641858816 (e-book) | ISBN 9781641857437 (hardcover) | ISBN 9781641858120 (paperback)
Subjects: LCSH: Rabbits--Infancy--Juvenile literature.
Classification: LCC QL737.L32 (ebook) | LCC QL737.L32 J66 2020 (print) | DDC 599.3213/92--dc23
LC record available at https://lccn.loc.gov/2018053614

Printed in the United States of America
Mankato, MN
May, 2019

About the Author

Kelsey Jopp is an editor, writer, and lifelong learner. She lives in Saint Paul, Minnesota, where she enjoys doing yoga and playing endless fetch with her sheltie, Teddy.

Table of Contents

nest

First Days

Bunnies are baby rabbits.

They are born in a **nest**.

They are very small.

They have pink skin.

This mother has
many bunnies.
They keep each
other warm.
The mother feeds them.

mother

Changes

Bunnies get older.

They grow **fur**.

They sleep a lot.

fur

Bunnies' ears open.

They can hear.

Their eyes open.

They can see.

ear
eye

Bunnies hop.

They move their **tails**.

They eat **grass**.

grass
tail

Growing Up

Bunnies keep growing.

They leave the nest.

They do not go back.

They live in groups.

Glossary

fur

nest

grass

tails

Index